Flying with Chinese

KA Workbook

Shuhan C. Wang, Ph. D. • Carol Ann Dahlberg, Ph. D.
Chiachyi Chiu, M.A. • Marisa Fang, M.S. • Mei-Ju Hwang, Ed.D.

© 2007 Marshall Cavendish International (Singapore) Private Limited

Published by Marshall Cavendish Education
A member of Times Publishing Limited
Times Centre, 1 New Industrial Road, Singapore 536196
Customer Service Hotline: (65) 6411 0820
E-mail: fps@sg.marshallcavendish.com
Website: www.marshallcavendish.com/education/sg

Distributed in North America by:

CHENG & TSUI COMPANY
Bringing Asia to the World™

Cheng & Tsui Company,
25 West St, Boston, MA 02111
www.cheng-tsui.com
Toll Free 1-800-554-1963

First published 2007

All rights reserved. No part of this publication may be reproduced, stored in a retrieval system or transmitted, in any form or by any means, electronic, mechanical, photocopying, recording or otherwise, without the prior permission of the copyright owner.

ISBN 978-981-01-6674-8

Publisher: Lim Geok Leng
Editors: Yvonne Lee   Richard Soh   Rita Teng   Jo Chiu   Chong Liping
Chief Designer: Roy Foo

Printed by Fabulous Printers Pte Ltd

Preface

Flying with Chinese is a series designed to make the most of children's natural ability to learn language by creating meaningful contexts for learning and guiding them towards language proficiency, literacy development and cultural appreciation. Each book is based on a theme and integrated with other subject areas in the elementary school curriculum.

Flying with Chinese is standards-based and focuses on learners' performance. Some of the important elements in this series include the following:
1. Thematic planning and instruction, with emphasis on the principles and structure of a good story;
2. "Standards for Chinese Language Learning," which is part of the *Standards for Foreign Language Learning in the 21st Century*;
3. Principles of *Understanding by Design*;
4. Matching languages with children (*Languages and Children: Making the Match*).

Under three umbrella themes, each book in the series takes on a different but related sub-theme. These themes are interesting to the learners, connect with the curriculum of the elementary school, promote understanding of Chinese culture, and provide a context for language use.

The Student Book provides the basic story for the lessons, while the Workbook gives learners the opportunity to practice the language and use the concepts presented in the Student Book. The Teacher Guide suggests activities for each day and indicates when the Workbook pages are to be used.

Flying with Chinese focuses on a group of children who are learning Chinese together. These children and their families come from a wide range of backgrounds, and several are heritage Chinese speakers. One member of the group goes to China with her family, where she attends a Chinese school and shares her experiences with her former classmates. Throughout the series learners are introduced to legends, real and fictional characters of importance to Chinese culture, and significant customs, celebrations, and other elements of the Chinese way of life.

Flying with Chinese can be used independently or as part of a sequence of study in a program. Just as a child can fly a kite on his own or in a group, we hope that children will have fun flying these Chinese kites while gaining insight into the Chinese-speaking world.

孙悟空来看我
Sun Wukong Comes to Visit Me

目录 Contents

Lesson 1	这是什么？What's This?	1
Lesson 2	石头在哪里？Where Is the Rock?	4
Lesson 3	你是谁？Who Are You?	7
Lesson 4	孙悟空学我！Sun Wukong Is Copying Me!	11
Lesson 5	你好！Hello!	14
Lesson 6	你会做什么？What Can You Do?	18
Lesson 7	我好饿！I Am Hungry!	21
Lesson 8	我要回家 I Want to Go Home	24
Lesson 9	孙悟空，再见！Good-bye, Sun Wukong!	29

第1课 这是什么？

妈妈，你看，这是什么？

啊，好奇怪的石头！

石头

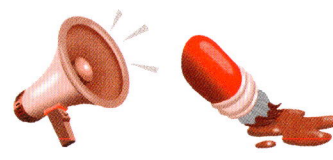# 好奇怪的石头

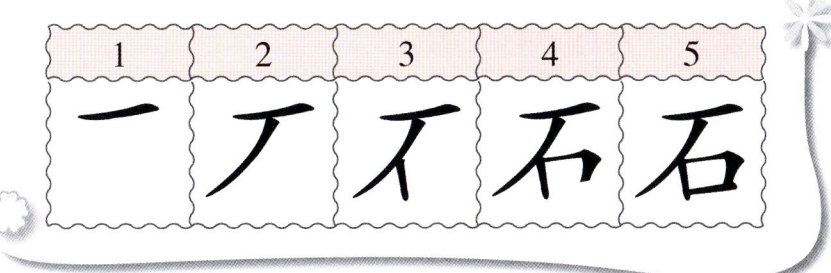

 **I can do these things in Chinese, can you?**

I can...

❖ ask what something is

❖ ask for permission

❖ recognize the *hanzi* "石", know what it means and how to say it

Date	Date

第2课 石头在哪里？

🔍 石头在哪里？

📢 ✏️ 石头在……

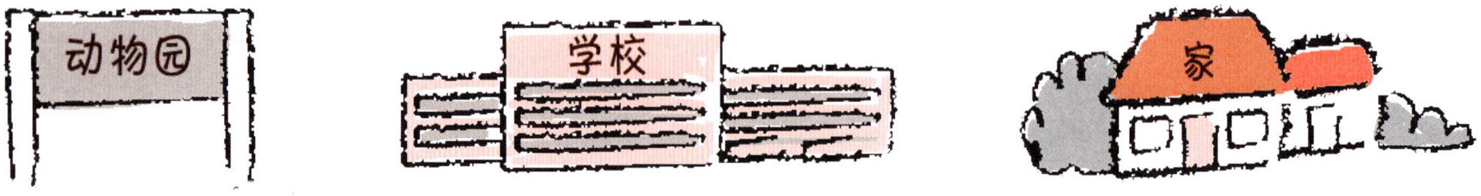

 小猴子,你是谁啊?

咦,哪里来的小猴子?

小猴子,你是谁啊?

 小

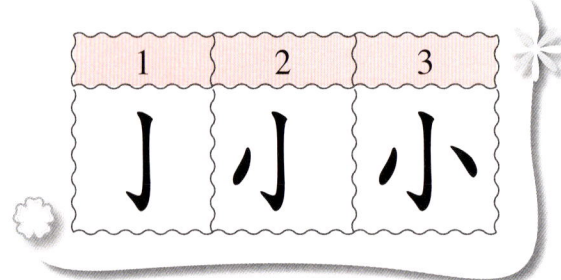

 **I can do these things in Chinese, can you?**

I can... Date   Date

❖ ask where something is

❖ ask who someone is

❖ sing the song "石头在哪里？" with the class

❖ recognize the *hanzi* "小", know what it means and how to say it

第3课　你是谁？

1. 你是谁？　我是……

2. 你是谁？　我是……

3. 你是谁？　我是……

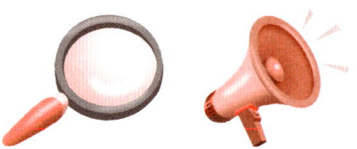 中国在哪里？

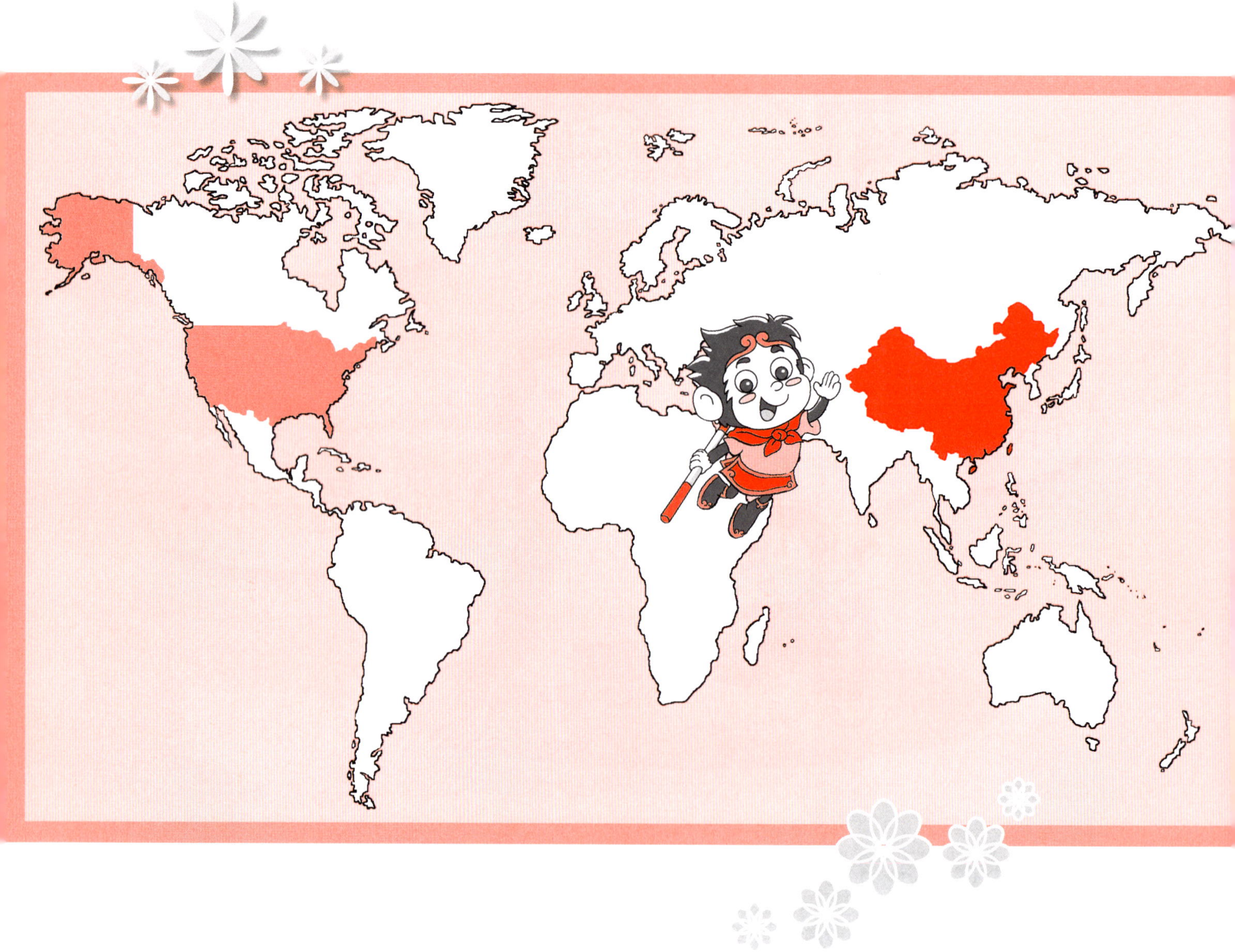

石头变成了谁？

1. 莉莉

2. 孙悟空

3. 莉莉的妈妈

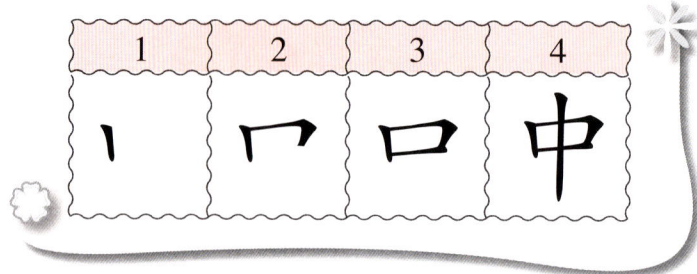

I can do these things in Chinese, can you?

I can...

    Date   Date

❖ tell who I am

❖ ask where someone comes from

❖ locate China on the globe or map

❖ tell someone that we be friends

❖ recognize the *hanzi* "中", know what it means and how to say it

第4课 孙悟空学我！

莉莉在做什么？

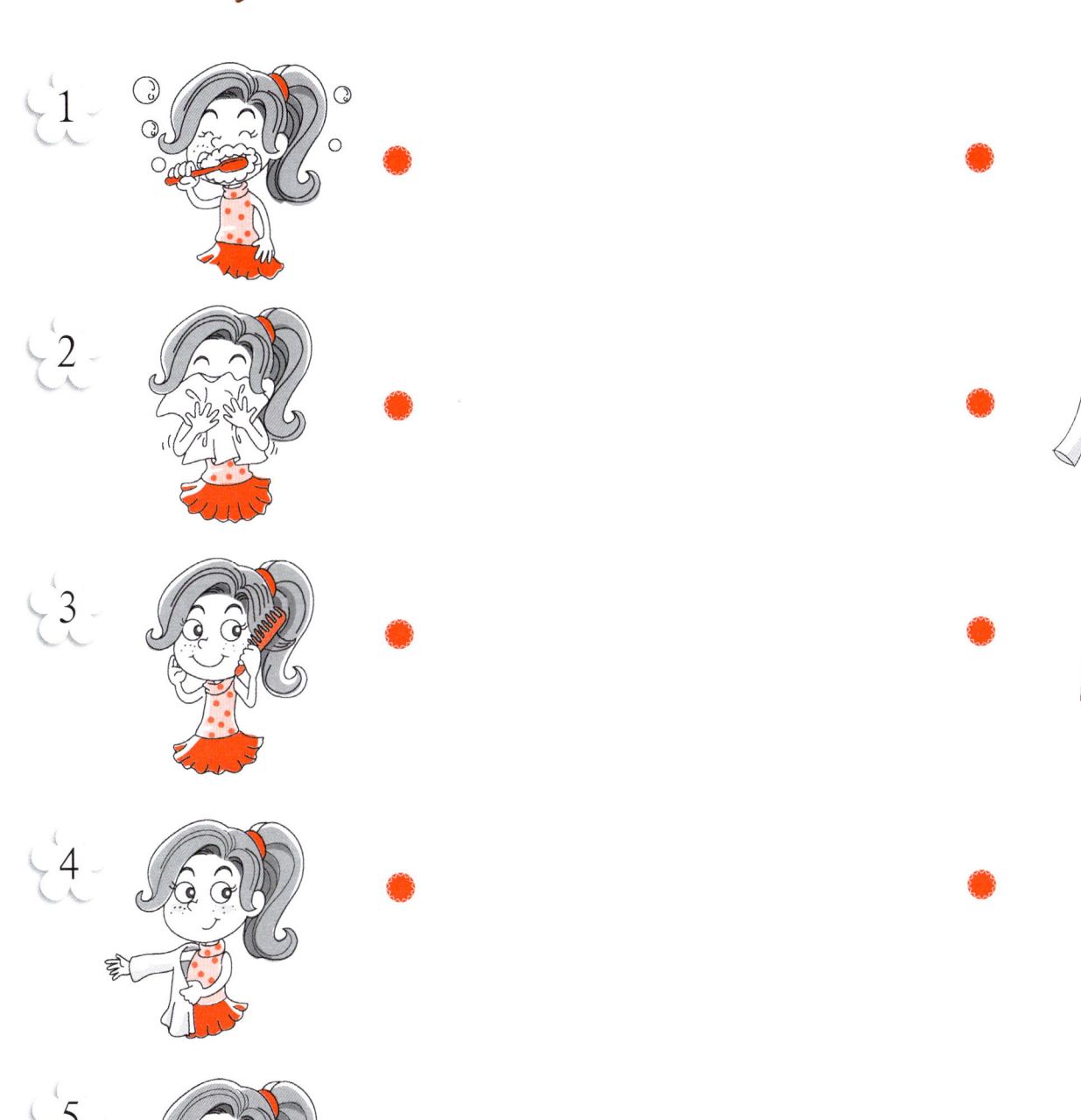

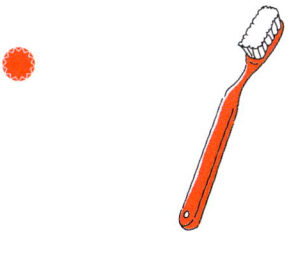

1 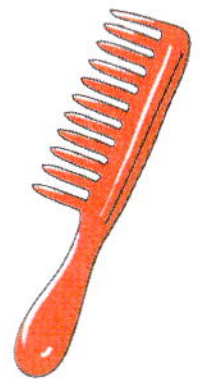
2 
3 
4
5

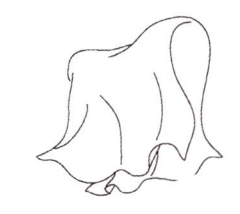

 孙悟空也在做什么？

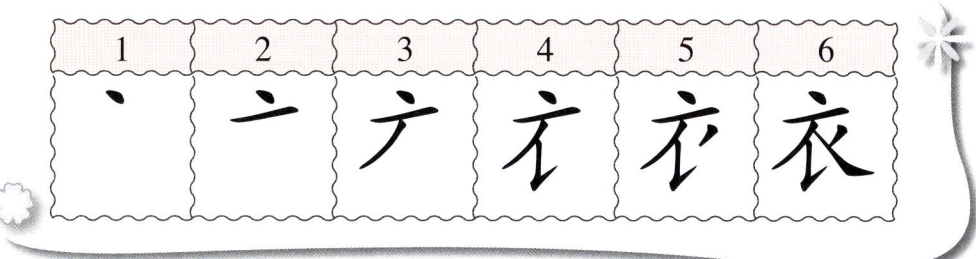

 **I can do these things in Chinese, can you?**

I can...   Date   Date

❖ follow the teacher's instructions to act out the daily routines

❖ tell and act out a morning routine

❖ tell I can do something too

❖ sing and act out the song "我们这样来刷牙" with the class

❖ recognize the *hanzi* "衣", know what it means and how to say it

第5课 你好！

1. 这是我的新朋友，他叫……

2. 这是我的新朋友，她叫……

3. 这是我们的新朋友，他叫……

莉莉向谁问好?

 新

1. 我的新朋友

2. 我的新衣服

3. 我的新书包

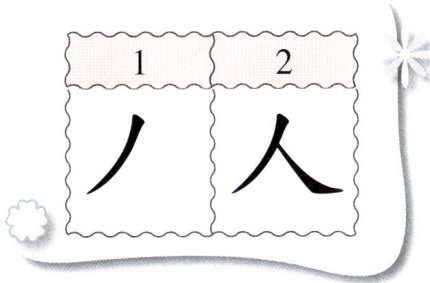

 **I can do these things in Chinese, can you?**

I can...　　　　　　　　　　　　　　Date　　Date

❖ greet and thank my teacher and friends

❖ introduce someone

❖ recognize the *hanzi* "人", know what it means and how to say it

第6课　你会做什么？

同学们会做什么？

1. 我会画画。 • •

2. 我会唱歌。 • •

3. 我会跳舞。 • •

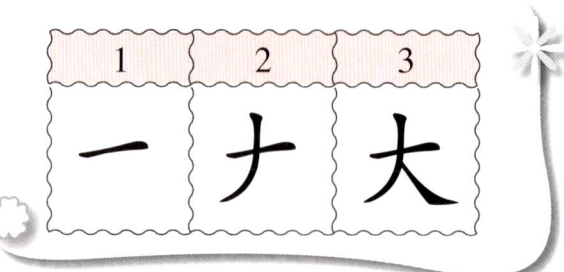

I can do these things in Chinese, can you?

I can...

- ❖ ask someone what they can do
- ❖ tell what I can do
- ❖ sing the song "一个拇指动一动" with the class
- ❖ recognize the *hanzi* "大", know what it means and how to say it

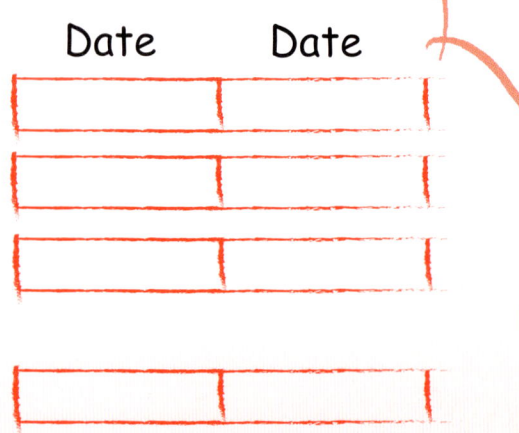

 # 第7课　我好饿！

 莉莉和孙悟空要去哪里？

 莉莉要去……
孙悟空要去……

家里　　厕所　　学校　　动物园

Rule: To make a turn when the path branches out.

 妈妈做什么？

1. 洗手　　2. 洗脸　　3. 洗衣服

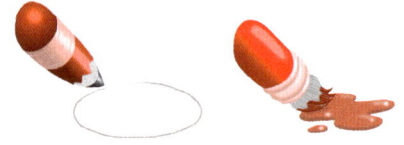  

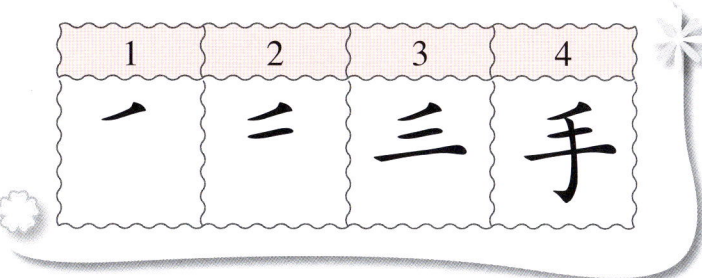

 **I can do these things in Chinese, can you?**

I can...   Date   Date

❖ tell someone that I'm hungry

❖ tell someone I need to go to the bathroom and wash my hands

❖ recognize the *hanzi* "手", know what it means and how to say it

第8课 我要回家

1. 你要吃香蕉吗? 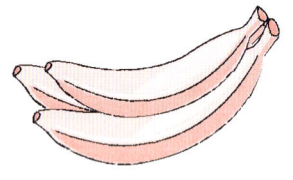   要   （不要）

2. 你要吃苹果吗?    要   不要

3. 你要喝水吗? 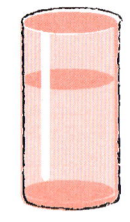   要   不要

4. 你要喝牛奶吗?    要   不要

  你要吃什么？

  你要喝什么？

 莉莉怎么了？

1.  莉莉生病了。

2.  莉莉饿了。

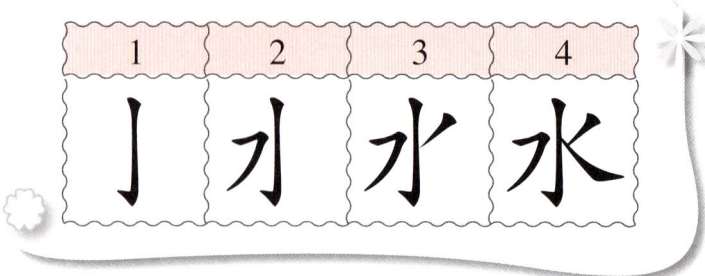

I can do these things in Chinese, can you?

I can... Date   Date

❖ offer something to eat or drink

❖ ask what's wrong

❖ say that I want to go home

❖ show my surprise in words

❖ sing the song "小猴子" with the class

❖ recognize the *hanzi* "水", know what it means and how to say it

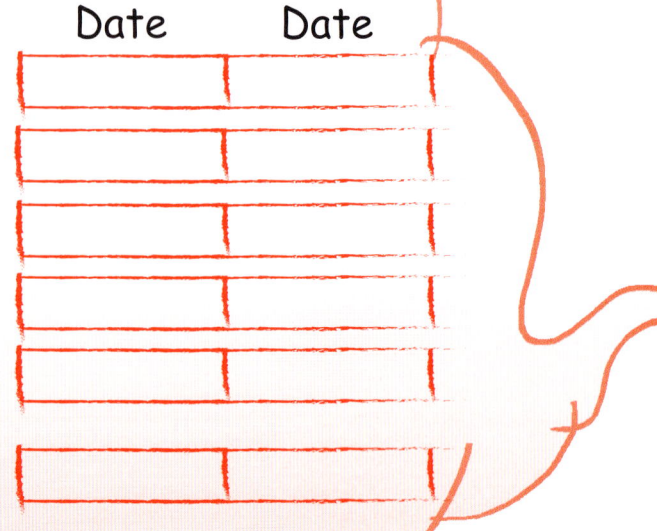

第9课 孙悟空，再见！

莉莉在说什么？

 我们一起……

1

2

3

上

1	2	3
丨	卜	上

下

1	2	3
一	丅	下

I can do these things in Chinese, can you?

I can...   Date   Date

❖ ask someone to come down

❖ tell things that I want to do with my friends

❖ explain what Sun Wukong wants to do

❖ say goodbye and ask my friends to come back to visit

❖ recognize the *hanzi* "上" and "下", know what they mean and how to say them

我

1

我

我叫＿＿＿＿＿＿＿。

3

我

我要吃＿＿＿＿＿＿。

5

我

我会＿＿＿＿＿＿。

7

我	我
我的朋友叫_____。 4	你好，这是我。 2
我	我
再见！ 8	我要喝_____。 6